Dregs

Also by Cynthia Cruz:

How the End Begins
Wunderkammer
The Glimmering Room
Ruin

Dregs

Cynthia Cruz

Four Way Books
Tribeca

Library of Congress Cataloging-in-Publication Data

Names: Cruz, Cynthia, author.
Title: Dregs / Cynthia Cruz.
Description: New York, NY : Four Way Books, [2018]
Identifiers: LCCN 2018003713 | ISBN 9781945588181 (pbk. : alk. paper)
Classification: LCC PS3603.R893 A6 2018 | DDC 811/.6--dc23
LC record available at https://lccn.loc.gov/2018003713

This book is manufactured in the United States of America and printed on acid-free paper.

Four Way Books is a not-for-profit literary press. We are grateful for the assistance we receive from individual donors, public arts agencies, and private foundations.

This publication is made possible with public funds from the National Endowment for the Arts

and from the New York State Council on the Arts, a state agency.

PROUD MEMBER

We are a proud member of the Community of Literary Magazines and Presses.

DREGS

1. The sediment of liquors; the more solid particles which settle at the bottom of a solution or other liquid; grounds, lees, feculent matters.
2. Feces, excrement, refuse, rubbish; corrupt or defiling matters.
3. The most worthless part or parts; the base or useless residue; the refuse or offscourings.
4. Last remains, small remnant, residue.

"One can speak of a writing sickness."

—Marguerite Duras

CONTENTS

THE ABANDONED LETTER

In this shimmering
I have found his voice.

Consider this:
He appeared to me

In the rich red wing
Of the Chinese Vault.

A ravishment,
When we met.

I will call this
A love song.

The perfume
Of his body, a damp

And flowering music.
Little circle of death

Among the love
Objects. In Paris

He takes my face
In his hands

And we vanish.

VINTAGE

All last winter
The windows sealed shut.

And the small, blue, magic
Plastic transistor

Playing Dory Previn,
A soft, silk ribbon

Unfolding
From its bolt.

WHAT MUSIC

The crop God promised.

That I could not.
I could not.

The cry of a small bird,
The bright red seed.

Now, I am
Even.

And the world
Comes quiet.

I hold the living
Book in my hands

Walking through the black
Fields and forest

To the glossy blue lake
Of the sea.

WILD IS THE WIND

Enter the diaphanous.
The ritual of rigging

Up your lame machinery.
Snow-blind of the mind.

Oh, my broken fox, my darling
Weak thing,

Lost in your dream,
Pretty, blonde gamine.

THE BRIEF ENACTMENT OF DARKNESS, WARPED WITH MEANING I

Keys and wooden birds.

Red toys and snow-
White plush,

Animals, stuffed: a doe, a foal,
And small blue and yellow birds.

My trophies, my proof.

BELL IN THE WATER

Darboven panels and a catalogue
Of stars. Or death.

Through the rush
Of newly driven snow.

Evening, I wander lakeside
Heavy with the tomb of sorrow

Dropped deep inside me.

Ephemera, and trauma.

I thought I could stop
The incessant hum

By moving from city
To city,

By starving clean
The body.

The miraculous leveling out
Of meaning.

Obsessive archiving and collecting
As a means to stop the tremulating drone

Of memory, the diamond-white
Rush of doom.

WILD LOVE

Here, in the First Church
Of Reverie, the sharp

Bell of memory
Ringing in the blinding white arc of noon.

Mistress, will you
Wait for me

Outside the gates.
Will you hold the river

Up for me,
So we can enter

Together
The way the dead do.

APRÈS COUP

First, the Mariinsky Ballet.

Then, winters of long warm baths
Linden, mandarin, and milk
Blossom.

The loss of God,

Odd little Rondelay,
Little box of sure,
White Belgium.

Curricula of having spent

What little was left
Of the money.

Loose, now, of God,
In a gown of white

Hissing flies, and sweet
Blonde mother,

Marianne, wrecked,
At the edge,

Glowing,
Bright vessel
Of Diazepam.

GHOST

The world is a Russian
Wood of wolves and white

Night foxes.
Danger,

And other,
Smaller figures.

My secret, my sweet
Fever,

Where among the shattered
Voices are you?

Glimmering white
Like a god, and living

Inside the jeweled
Prison of your mind.

Lies and the bell
Of death.

Miraculous, your face,
Forever changed

By the sickening poverty
Of sorrow.

APRÈS COUP

Now I hear the good voices.

Go, they say, to the holy place,
The sick child dying in the barn.

This is the vocabulary of killing.

All of this waiting
For the world to begin.

THE WINTER MUSEUM

White minks kept in glass cages,
And their otherworldly hum.

The simplicity of doom,
Its domestic strain,

A perfect and frozen
Akhmatova winter.

The cathedral of harms:
Death

And her bright white
Flower-like wings.

Please, don't remove me
From this blue kingdom.

The world and her
Sting,

This incoherent dream
Being played on a record.

THE DEAD SERIOUS GAME

In the small blonde dacha in the snow
We undress,

We drink the cold
Wine we've been given.

With scissors and glue,
Bits of ripped cloth,

Blue and silver thread
We make toys for the dying.

Figures in gold,
Small colts, and dancing ballet dolls.

This is the dream
Vocabulary.

This is the end.

THE HOUR OF THE STAR

In the blue séance room
Beneath the stacked chandelier,

The miracle of sorrow, or
Milk and stars.

The deep
Key of death.

A black
Error on the edge

Of the tall
Blonde field.

And no one knows
Where that besieged city is.

But to go back
To that

Little town and be born,
Again.

DREGS

Grab the blankets,
The whiskey and pálinka.

I'll build us a boat made of money and warp.

Honey, and the dark fugue
Of foreboding.

Pack the song, dirty in its drone,
Its filthy doom

In a jar of black
Blood, and crushed
With snow.

Please
Don't let me go.

The boat,
It will take us

To the sweet
And filthy water,

The murky
Forever

Of death's
Endless slumber.

TAGEBÜCHER

For Eva Hesse

Decadent, glass cells
Like a hive.

Or Eva Hesse, fevering
The electric divine.

I'm going back
To where I came from.

It no longer exists.

Lost like dust
Inside my little America.

In the night
Thieves come by

Carrying filth and disease
Inside their small gold boxes.

MASQUERADE

Take the sheared
Mink coat off,

The soft pink
Silk shift;

Black lace stockings,
Soft

Black leather
Ballet flats,

The long-sleeved,
Voluminous dress.

Wash the miraculous
Make-up off:

Cream Matte
Face base.

Powder, liner,
Stardust.

Remove the crystal
Chandelier

Earrings, gold
Bangles.

Light the Italian
Blood orange candle.

Take the yellow
Triple-tiered lemon

Cream cake
From the icebox.

And let the spell
Of God's sweet orchestra

Finally
Enter me.

WINTER

In a locked room,
In a hotel downtown, the black

Telephone ringing without stop.
If I say anything, I will vanish.

Inside the palace, I am afraid
To enter it: the cattails, the ink
Black shellac of it.

Mother, she had a vision:
Tiny, semi-precious kingdom.

Why am I
Always crawling the never
Ending hallway

Into the dead end's
Ink black dot.

SELF PORTRAIT WITH FACE COVERED IN TINY WHITE DIAMONDS

I wrote the Book
Of the End,

Charting its movements
Like a weather.

I listened to its white
Annihilating music,

And was lowered slowly down,
Into the sickly sweet

Specter of childhood,
Its thick white cream

Of regret. The black
Boat of death, just a dot,

Moving slowly
Toward the shore.

SPELL BIND

I cannot
Be away from him.

My Argonaut,
My wild flock

Of bright red
Crimson.

Feeding me
His sweet and golden fruit.

NOTEBOOK ON DISINTEGRATION

Then the habit of breaking
Glass, and the trick of burning.

Spangles, and weeping.

The bright red germ
Of pomp and ceremony.

A room of silver flowers, water, and a black
Plastic radio set back to zero.

NATURE MORT

Bathing his godly body
In a white tub of ice.

Damage, and a petrol
Of dead black flowers.

The sweet pollution
Of what God he thought

He took in.
Hustler of the glossy edge,

Bright germ of dreg
Searing its way

Through the blue cathedral
Of his mind.

DRECK

The peonies in the porcelain
Nod off

As the white lamp
Of the moon

Moves
Into your world.

Your luminous body
Beneath the clean white sheets.

Pretty mystery,
Let the bright germ

Of madness
Devour me

Entirely. Like a thought,
Repeating,

I cannot stop.

BLAU VOGEL

A German winter weeps
Inside me.

Yellowing,
Like a death rattle.

In the game of death,
You take the mystical

Medicine, and pray
It hustles you

Away from the silvering
Edge.

DEATH CERTIFICATE

What exactly am I looking for
In this desert, this
Dead city?

Dazed, I live inside
My vast memory cages.

I lick, pace, and gaze here.

They say she followed the song
Of her voices.

But, she died in a fire
Just like Bachmann.

THE SILVER CRADLE

Rode in a golden Benz
Into the silver scrim.

Cells, dust, and scum.
Love, my dumb and fevering fox

The black sin of fear,
Singed deep inside us.

RED ALMANAC

A flame in the forest
The fire bird circles

Whispering, the water
Is a wound.

The blind white foxes,
They are afraid of everything.

Their sadness is a wordless
Song, a miraculous

Cacophony of warm
Liquid amber and music,

A doorless darkness.

HOTEL BERLIN

In the rooms of a rundown palace
You said, Ruined. You said, Princess.

You said nothing to me
For three long weeks.

The color of that room
Is eel black.

When I was a girl and still
German, I stood alone

At the end of the sea.
You may have loved me then.

I sent a message through the cages
Of a great whale's teeth.

For three weeks, I did not sleep.
I set jars of sweet milk and baskets

Of bright berries and red
Marmalade outside your door.

In the dream
Where you come to me

I kiss your mouth
Tasting the secret

Letters of your history.
I swear

Somewhere in Siberia
A godly ocean of bison

Still roam free.
You, kneeling before me,

In this,
The last and final room.

SNOW DIARY

If I use cellophane and diazotype

I just might disintegrate.

This isn't a diary entry or proof.

I don't remember.

But there are photographs.

Then, the film goes blank.

The elsewhere of death

Its blinding

White salve—

HEIMWEH (or NOSTALGIA)

I'm not afraid of what they
Will do to me.

They can take away everything and still
I'm free.

Insane, even, or with the wrong music.

I went mad trying to come back home again.

Walking along the LA Expressway
With my bright plastic bags and medicine.

But now it is finally inside me.

The warm white purr
Of his sweet music.

SELF PORTRAIT: LAKE CONSTANCE

In the vast garden
Outside grandmother's mansion

Under the willow
Near the aviary

Eating pastries from their small pink
Paper boxes.

Wearing dead
Marianne's fox fur.

I listen
As God slowly begins.

LEILA

Just a breath, the white palace of your death
In the smallest of beds in Cairo.

I ate a single boiled egg
In seven days

To mourn
The memory of you.

Of soldiers,
There are always too many.

In olive costume, their pretty
Black boots

Click inside the locked white dream
Of my sleep.

THE BRIEF ENACTMENT OF DARKNESS, WARPED WITH MEANING II

A bee-like drone.
The pretty parade of illness.

A kill here, a dark smudge there.
The sweet, yellow rattle of death.

No one knows
When this will stop.

Milk on the tongue.

How then can I not vanish?

All of this splendoring and promiscuous.

Then, the film is a blank screen.

There is no sunlight left.

LITTLE AMERICA

Girlhood, locked inside a wire box.
At thirteen, she was mute.
The LA doctors watched
Truffaut's *Wild Child* for clues
On how to cure the feral girl.
Reporters and neighbors warmed
To the story, camped outside the girl's home,
Stood on the dead, brown lawn.
Then, went. Pulled the string marked, Next.

ORIGIN

And I will glue and wire
The smashed contraption
Of my mind back:
Pretty blonde skater trash.

Anxiety is mystical, it
Feeds on me.
And no, I don't
Think I can make it

Stop. High priestess, lead me
Back beneath the warm
Brine-like glittering,

Underwater spit of the mind's
Sweet unraveling.

WHITE ROOM

In the sanitarium, starving
Simone Weil, and transported
By ambulance.

What a beautiful room, she said,
To die in.

Delirious, on her deathbed,
Listing off the miraculous
Banquet of her childhood.

French bread, and butter
Soup, mashed potatoes,
Roast lamb in mint,
Thick cream, and fruit tarts
Made by her mother, with milk.

But, where
Does God live?

Her last words
On this earth
Was *Nurses.*

POST SCRIPT

A little moment of pretty
Outside Bemelmans.

Honey, my sweet
Magic and fever,

In cream silk suit.
Glimmering

On the pavement
Like a girl.

FORGOTTEN GLOSSES

In a room of blonde wood,
A pack of cigarettes, and a red

Cosmetics case packed with amber
Bottles of medicine.

The remainders of childhood:
Music and blue

And white porcelain. A paper mask
Of cat's face,

With whiskers, and a soft ribbon
That fastens below the chin.

Outside, the golden
Mercedes waits:

My sweet boat
Of death—

What was I saying?

The mind goes blank.

NEUKÖLN

An astrological error,
The night I came into this world.

It was ice cold, December,
The tail end of winter.

When father died,
Mother vanished into her room,

His heart in a gold jar.
And she never returned.

SILENCER

Sorrow in the black strip of film,
The static of the television set.

Delicate glass vase filled with flowers.

Telepathy, phenomena.

I wanted to make a star-like cluster of sticky jewels
Inside a veil of indescribable music.

I wanted the work to die
Inside me.

Like a Tarkovsky, or Béla Tarr movie.

Delicate, paper cutouts made as children.
Or masks made with paper plates and white string

To hide the face behind.

All great works, they say, have death
Inside their making.

THE LAST FILM IN THE WORLD

The black panorama
Of poverty,

Its warm lies and death.

Its liquor stores and detritus.

The fevering ghost
Of compulsion:

Whiskey, death, or the book.

I cannot stop—

The music is a feral, silver milk.

It is my filthy home.

I walk to the broken gates
And enter—

Acknowledgments

The Academy of American Poets Poem-a-Day, Coldfront, Drunken Boat, Field, Guernica, The Kenyon Review online, *Like Starlings, The Literary Review, Nat-Brut, No Tokens, Paris-American, Plume,* and *West Branch.*

Cynthia Cruz is the author of five collections of poetry, including four with Four Way Books: *The Glimmering Room* (2012), *Wunderkammer* (2014), and *How the End Begins* (2016). Cruz has received fellowships from Yaddo and the MacDowell Colony as well as a Hodder Fellowship from Princeton University. She has an MFA from Sarah Lawrence College in writing and an MFA in Art Criticism & Writing from the School of Visual Arts. Cruz is currently pursuing a PhD in German Studies at Rutgers University. She teaches at Sarah Lawrence College.

Publication of this book was made possible by grants and donations. We are also grateful to those individuals who participated in our 2017 Build a Book Program. They are:

Anonymous (6), Evan Archer, Sally Ball, Vincent Bell, Jan Bender-Zanoni, Zeke Berman, Kristina Bicher, Laurel Blossom, Carol Blum, Betsy Bonner, Mary Brancaccio, Lee Briccetti, Deirdre Brill, Anthony Cappo, Carla & Steven Carlson, Caroline Carlson, Stephanie Chang, Tina Chang, Liza Charlesworth, Paula Colangelo, Maxwell Dana, Machi Davis, Marjorie Deninger, Emily Flitter, Lukas Fauset, Monica Ferrell, Jennifer Franklin, Donna Thagard & Helen Fremont, Martha Webster & Robert Fuentes, Chuck Gillett, Dorothy Goldman, Dr. Lauri Grossman, Naomi Guttman & Jonathan Mead, Steven Haas, Mary & John Heilner, Hermann Hesse, Deming Holleran, Nathaniel Hutner, Janet Jackson, Christopher Kempf, David Lee, Jen Levitt, Howard Levy, Owen Lewis, Paul Lisicky, Sara London & Dean Albarelli, David Long, Katie Longofono, Cynthia Lowen, Ralph & Mary Ann Lowen, Donna Masini, Louise Mathias, Catherine McArthur, Nathan McClain, Victoria McCoy, Gregory McDonald, Britt Melewski, Kamilah Moon, Carolyn Murdoch, Rebecca & Daniel Okrent, Tracey Orick, Zachary Pace, Gregory Pardlo, Allyson Paty, Veronica Patterson, Marcia & Chris Pelletiere, Maya Pindyck, Taylor Pitts, Eileen Pollack, Barbara Preminger, Kevin Prufer, Vinode Ramgopal, Martha Rhodes, Peter & Jill Schireson, Roni & Richard Schotter, Andrew Seligsohn, Soraya Shalforoosh, Peggy Shinner, James Snyder & Krista Fragos, Alice St. Claire-Long, Megan Staffel, Robin Taylor, Marjorie & Lew Tesser, Boris Thomas, Judith Thurman, Susan Walton, Calvin Wei, Abby Wender, Bill Wenthe, Allison Benis White, Elizabeth Whittlesey, Hao Wu, Monica Youn, and Leah Zander.